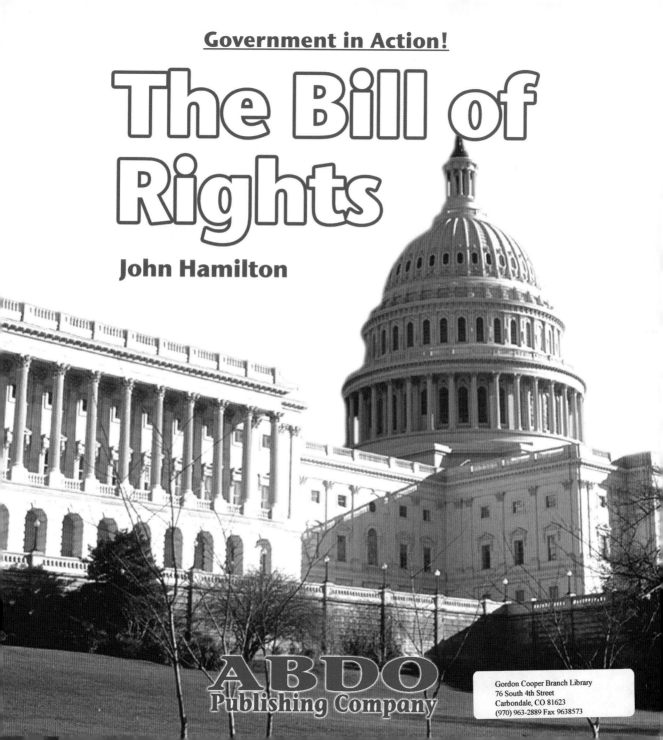

The Bill of Rights

John Hamilton

ABDO
Publishing Company

visit us at
www.abdopub.com

Published by ABDO Publishing Company, 4940 Viking Drive, Edina, Minnesota 55435.
Copyright © 2005 by Abdo Consulting Group, Inc. International copyrights reserved in all
countries. No part of this book may be reproduced in any form without written permission from the
publisher. The Checkerboard Library™ is a trademark and logo of ABDO Publishing Company.

Printed in the United States.

Cover Photos: Corbis
Interior Photos: AP/Wide World p. 28; Corbis pp. 1, 8, 9, 11, 12, 13, 14, 15, 20, 24, 25, 27, 31;
    Fotosearch p. 29; Getty Images pp. 22, 23; Index Stock p. 24; Library of Congress pp. 5, 18;
    North Wind pp. 7, 19, 21

Series Coordinator: Kristin Van Cleaf
Editors: Jennifer R. Krueger, Kristin Van Cleaf
Art Direction & Maps: Neil Klinepier

Library of Congress Cataloging-in-Publication Data

Hamilton, John, 1959-
    The Bill of Rights / John Hamilton.
        p. cm. -- (Government in action!)
    Includes index.
    ISBN 1-59197-643-X
    1. United States. Constitution. 1st-10th Amendments--Juvenile literature. 2. Constitutional
amendments--United States--Juvenile literature. 3. Civil rights--United States--Juvenile literature.
[1. United States. Constitution. 1st-10th Amendments. 2. Constitutional amendments--United
States. 3. Civil rights.] I. Title. II. Government in action! (ABDO Publishing Company).

KF4750.H26 2004
342.7308'5--dc22
                                                                    2003063615

Contents

The Bill of Rights

The American colonists fought for their freedom from England nearly 200 years ago. After they won, they were free to create their own government. They soon wrote the U.S. Constitution to define this government.

However, the Constitution did not include many **guarantees** of personal freedoms. For this reason, James Madison helped adopt ten amendments to the Constitution. They became known as the Bill of Rights.

The Bill of Rights is a document that explains the rights of U.S. citizens. It guarantees those rights and limits the power of the federal government. Today, the U.S. judicial system is built upon these rights.

Americans today have freedom of speech, the press, and religion. They can gather in peaceful groups in public. All people are guaranteed a fair trial. They have all these freedoms because of the Bill of Rights.

Opposite page: *The original Bill of Rights*

Congress OF THE United States,

begun and held at the City of New York, on

Wednesday, the fourth of March, one thousand, seven hundred and eighty nine.

THE _____

RESOLVED _____

ARTICLES _____

Article the first. _____

Article the second. _____

Article the third. _____

Article the fourth. _____

Article the fifth. _____

Article the sixth. _____

Article the seventh. _____

Article the eighth. _____

Article the ninth. _____

Article the tenth. _____

Article the eleventh. _____

Article the twelfth. _____

ATTEST,

Frederick Augustus Muhlenberg, *Speaker of the House of Representatives.*

John Adams, *Vice President of the United States, and President of the Senate.*

Leading to War

For many years, Britain controlled 13 colonies in North America. Over time, the colonists grew more and more independent. They were soon ready for freedom from England.

The British won the **French and Indian War** in 1763. At this point, they wanted to tighten their control over the colonies. The war had cost England a lot of money. The government decided the colonies should help pay part of the cost.

So, Britain issued new laws and taxes. One such tax was the Stamp Act of 1765. It forced colonists to buy special stamps to put on legal documents and newspapers. The colonists protested that the tax was unfair.

But other taxes followed, including one on tea. The colonists began **boycotting** British goods. Then on December 16, 1773, colonists sneaked onto ships in Boston Harbor in Massachusetts. They dumped a shipment of British tea into the water. This incident became known as the Boston Tea Party.

As punishment for the Boston Tea Party, the English closed Boston Harbor and limited the government of Massachusetts. And, they passed the **Quartering Act**. The colonists called the laws the Intolerable Acts. They believed their freedoms were being taken away, and they were ready to fight for them.

Colonists revolt against the Stamp Act in Boston, Massachusetts.

Independence

Fighting soon broke out all over the colonies. On April 19, 1775, the colonists and the English fought each other at the Battles of Lexington and Concord near Boston, Massachusetts. This was the beginning of the Revolutionary War.

The colonists banded together in a temporary government. The leaders soon decided the colonies should be independent. Five men worked to create a document. They were John Adams, Roger Sherman, Benjamin Franklin, Robert Livingston, and Thomas Jefferson.

On July 4, 1776, the men finished the Declaration of Independence. They wrote that government should exist only to protect the rights of the people. These rights included "Life, Liberty and the pursuit of Happiness." The declaration also stated that the colonies were now a country separate from England.

A statue in Concord, Massachusetts, honors the minutemen. These men fought against the British in the Battle of Concord.

The fighting continued. Eight years later, England finally recognized the colonists' independence. The two sides signed a peace treaty on September 3, 1783. The colonies were now 13 separate states.

Benjamin Franklin, John Adams, and Thomas Jefferson write the Declaration of Independence.

Confederation

During the Revolutionary War, the colonists created the Articles of **Confederation**. It created a loose union of states. The people didn't want another powerful central government that had control over their personal rights. So, the articles gave the state governments more power than the central government.

The central government was the Confederation Congress. It had a number of powers. It could declare war, sign treaties, and create and borrow money. The state governments had the power to control trade, raise taxes, enforce laws, and carry out justice.

Unfortunately, the limits on the central government led to problems. It could not enforce laws once they were passed. As a result, many states ignored or canceled a number of laws. In addition, there was no national court system.

The Confederation Congress couldn't collect taxes or control foreign trade. This meant the government could not pay its **debts**. The states also didn't work very closely together. They started taxing goods from their neighbors.

Opposite page: *After the war, many people had trouble with debt. As a result, in 1786 and 1787, Massachusetts farmers revolted in Shays's Rebellion.*

The **Confederation** Congress did not have enough power. It could not prevent or solve both its own problems and troubles between states. Political leaders soon realized that without changes, the new country would not last.

A New Government

George Washington leads the delegates as they debate during the Constitutional Convention.

People in the states knew the Articles of **Confederation** had to change. So on May 25, 1787, state delegates met at the Pennsylvania State House in Philadelphia. Rhode Island was the only state that did not send delegates.

The meeting at the State House became known as the Constitutional **Convention**. The delegates' purpose was to improve the current central government. But soon, the men realized this would be too difficult. Instead they wrote a new document, the U.S. Constitution.

The men elected George Washington as president of the **convention**. Some other important men who participated were Benjamin Franklin, Alexander Hamilton, James Madison, and John Dickinson. The delegates had several plans for the new government. For example, James Madison helped come up with the Virginia Plan. It separated the federal government into three parts. The parts included the executive, legislative, and judicial branches. They would all share power.

George Washington was a general during the Revolutionary War. He was also the first president of the United States.

The smaller states didn't like the Virginia Plan. They favored the New Jersey Plan instead. It would give the **Confederation** Congress power to raise taxes and control trade. It would also give the central government more power to enforce the laws it created.

The delegates **debated** these and other plans. They needed to solve a number of issues. One of the biggest was states' representation in the legislature. The large states wanted representation to be determined by each state's population. The small states thought each state should have an equal number of representatives.

Eventually, the **convention** members agreed upon the Connecticut Compromise. It said that each state would have the same number of senators. Representation in the House of Representatives would be based on population.

Oliver Ellsworth was a lawyer from Connecticut who helped create the Connecticut Compromise.

The delegates prepare to sign the final draft of the new Constitution.

In September, the delegates finally finished their work. They had created a government with three branches based on the Virginia Plan. On September 17, 1787, the men met for the last time. Thirty-nine of the 55 delegates signed the new Constitution. Now it was time to get the states' approval.

Adding the Bill

Before the Constitution could take effect, nine of the 13 states had to **ratify** it. The people immediately began **debating** the new document. Those in favor of the new government were called Federalists. Those against it were called Anti-Federalists.

Newspapers in the states printed the opinions of both sides. Many Anti-Federalists did not like that the central government would have so much power. One of their biggest complaints was that the Constitution did not include a bill of rights.

Most of the delegates thought individuals' rights would be protected by the states. But many Americans did not think this was good enough. They believed that the government should be forbidden from taking away a citizen's rights. This way, it could not misuse its power as England had.

The two sides continued to debate. A few states voted to ratify the Constitution, but not enough to officially approve the new government. The Federalists became worried.

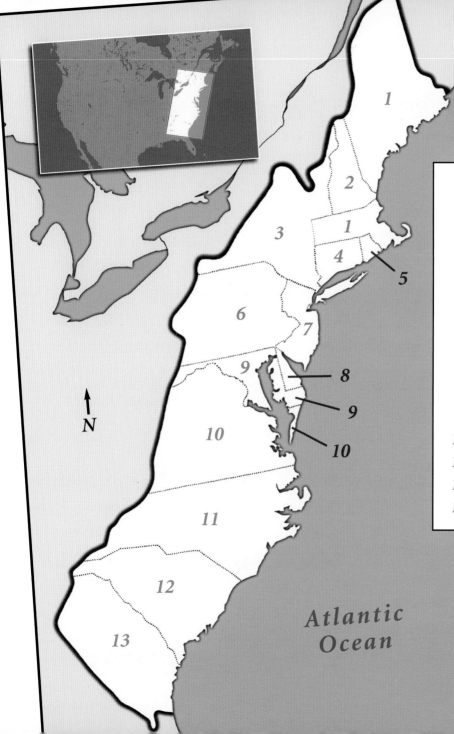

The 13 Original States

1 – Massachusetts
2 – New Hampshire
3 – New York
4 – Connecticut
5 – Rhode Island
6 – Pennsylvania
7 – New Jersey
8 – Delaware
9 – Maryland
10 – Virginia
11 – North Carolina
12 – South Carolina
13 – Georgia

N

Atlantic Ocean

Many states would **ratify** the Constitution only if a bill of rights was added. Eventually, the Federalists agreed. At this point, more states voted for ratification. On June 21, 1788, New Hampshire was the ninth state to approve the Constitution.

James Madison was also convinced that a bill of rights was important. As one of Virginia's House representatives, he introduced 17 amendments at the first meeting of Congress in 1789. The lawmakers accepted 12 of them that September.

On October 2, President George Washington sent each of the states a copy of the amendments. By December 15, 1791, three-fourths of the states had ratified ten of the amendments. Today, they are known to Americans as the Bill of Rights.

An article announcing that Virginia has ratified the Constitution

James Madison

James Madison is often called the Father of the Constitution. He was born on March 16, 1751, and grew up on a plantation in Virginia. Madison studied at the College of New Jersey, which is now Princeton University. Later he studied politics, history, and law.

In 1776, Madison worked with Thomas Jefferson to write Virginia's constitution. He later used these laws as a model for the Virginia Plan at the Constitutional Convention. During the debates over ratification, he worked with Alexander Hamilton and John Jay to write the Federalist papers in support of the Constitution. Madison also helped add a bill of rights to the document.

Madison served as president from 1809 to 1817. After this, he ran a farm in Virginia. He spoke out against slavery and helped Jefferson create the University of Virginia. Over his last few years, Madison was ill and spent much time in bed. Still, he wrote many essays on government topics. He died in 1836.

The Amendments

The Bill of Rights is still an important part of U.S. **democracy**. It **guarantees** many of the rights characteristic of the United States. These ten amendments are the center of an American's liberties. And, they are the basis for the country's judicial system.

Amendment I

The First Amendment protects freedom of religion, speech, and the press. This protection allows Americans to choose their

religion. They can speak their minds without fear of punishment. Under the First Amendment, citizens can also gather in groups and **petition** the government.

These Muslim schoolgirls are free to practice their religion because of the First Amendment.

The colonists formed militias to defend themselves during the Revolutionary War.
As a result, many thought this was an important civil right.

Amendment II

The Second Amendment keeps the government from restricting a **militia**. In order to do this, the amendment allows citizens to carry guns. The **Founding Fathers** believed the ability to form militias was necessary. Today, many people **debate** whether citizens should still carry guns.

Amendment III

The Third Amendment states that the government can't house soldiers in citizens' homes without permission. This amendment was created to prevent laws such as the **Quartering Act** from being passed again.

Amendment IV

The Fourth Amendment protects citizens from unreasonable search and seizure by the police. This means that the police cannot search a citizen's home unless they have the proper papers from a judge.

Amendment V

The Fifth Amendment states that no one can be punished without **due process** of law. It forbids the government from trying a citizen twice for the same crime. A person also can't be forced to testify against him- or herself in a trial. And, people must be paid if their property is taken for public use.

A man on trial pleads his Fifth Amendment right to not testify against himself.

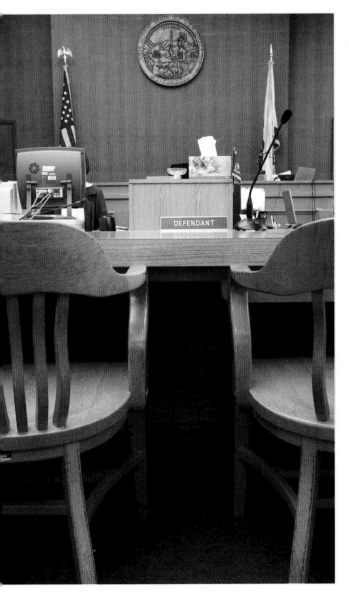

Amendment VI

The Sixth Amendment states that anyone accused of a crime has "the right to a speedy and public trial . . ." Citizens also have a right to a fair jury. They can confront the person or people accusing them. The Sixth Amendment gives people the right to a lawyer, as well.

Amendment VII

The Seventh Amendment **guarantees** a trial by jury in civil cases where the amount in dispute is more than $20.

Americans are guaranteed many rights when accused of a crime. An accused person is innocent until proven guilty.

Amendment VIII

The Eighth Amendment protects citizens arrested for a crime. It forbids the government from using violence during questioning. It also keeps the government from setting **bail** too high, which would be unfair to people with little money.

The Eighth Amendment protects citizens who are already in jail.

Amendment IX

The Ninth Amendment explains that people have more rights than those mentioned in the Constitution. The discussed rights are not more important than any other and cannot be used to deny other rights. For example, judges have ruled that the Ninth Amendment gives people the right to privacy.

Just one of an American's rights is to be tried by a jury.

Amendment X

The Tenth Amendment explains the division of power in the Constitution. It states that power not given to the federal government belongs to the states or the people.

The Ninth and Tenth Amendments protect people's general rights. This way, their freedom is not limited to what is mentioned in the other amendments.

The Bill in Action

The Bill of Rights is a basic part of the U.S. legal system. Over the years, the **Supreme Court** has ruled on many cases dealing with citizens' basic rights.

In 1963, the case *Abington Township v. Schempp* concerned Pennsylvania students who were required to read verses from the Bible during school. The Court ruled that this was against the First Amendment's separation of church and state.

Another example occurred in 1965. That year, two students were suspended because they had worn black armbands in school in order to protest the Vietnam War. The students fought back. In 1969, the Court's decision in *Tinker v. Des Moines* ruled that wearing the armbands was an act of freedom of speech protected by the First Amendment.

In *Gideon v. Wainwright,* a man charged with breaking and entering didn't have the money to hire a lawyer. But, the court refused to appoint him one. The Supreme Court ruled in 1963 that, under the Sixth Amendment, Gideon had a right to a court-appointed attorney. It was important to **guarantee** a fair trial.

In the 1961 case *Mapp v. Ohio,* the police searched a woman's home without the proper warrant. This document is required by the Fourth Amendment. The **Supreme Court** ruled that when items are taken this way they cannot be used as evidence in a court trial.

Mary Beth and John Tinker hold the armbands they wore to protest the Vietnam War. The Supreme Court ruled the bands were a form of free speech. So, the students could not be punished for wearing them.

Responsibilities

After the Constitutional **Convention** ended on September 17, 1787, Benjamin Franklin talked to a friend. She asked him what kind of government the **Founding Fathers** had created. He told her, "A republic, madam, if you can keep it."

Students learn about involvement in government while taking a tour of the statehouse in Des Moines, Iowa.

The Bill of Rights is important to the United States's **democratic** society. It **guarantees** and protects Americans' freedoms. But, along with these rights come personal responsibilities.

The United States is a democracy. That means citizens hold power. They have a responsibility to take an active part in their government. Many citizens do this by voting, running for office, or by simply learning about their government.

*Students visit the
Colorado State Capitol.*

The Bill of Rights protects the freedoms Americans need in order to be responsible citizens. Such freedoms allow the people to educate themselves. They have helped citizens keep this government by the people for more than 200 years.

Glossary

bail - the temporary release of a prisoner in exchange for money or other guarantee that the prisoner will attend trial. Bail avoids punishing a person who may be innocent, and it allows him or her to prepare a defense.

boycott - to refuse to deal with a person, store, or organization until they agree to certain conditions.

Confederation - a group united for support or common action.

convention - a large meeting set up for a special purpose.

debate - to discuss a question or topic, often publicly.

debt - something owed to someone, usually money.

democracy - a governmental system in which the people vote on how to run their country.

due process - legal proceedings carried out to follow established laws.

Founding Fathers - the men who attended the Constitutional Convention in Philadelphia in 1787. They helped write the Constitution.

French and Indian War - from 1754 to 1763. A series of battles fought for control of land in North America. England and its colonies fought against France, its colonies, and several Native American tribes.

guarantee - to make sure or certain.

militia - a group of citizens trained to fight in war or emergencies.

petition - to make a formal request to a person of authority.

Quartering Act - an act passed in 1765 that ordered colonists to supply British soldiers with food, drink, housing, fuel, and transportation. It expired in 1770, but it was revived again in 1774.

ratify - to officially approve.

Supreme Court - the highest, most powerful court in the United States.

Web Sites

To learn more about the Bill of Rights, visit ABDO Publishing Company on the World Wide Web at **www.abdopub.com**. Web sites about the Bill of Rights are featured on our Book Links page. These links are routinely monitored and updated to provide the most current information available.

The 10th Amendment

"The powers not delegated to the United States by the Constitution, nor prohibited by it to the States, are reserved to the States respectively, or to the people."

Index